July 2021

Snow Telos

Presentation by *BookLeaf Publishing*

Web: www.bookleafpub.com

E-mail: info@bookleafpub.com

ISBN: 9789363301269

First edition 2024

*To the dreamers and the escapists who just
want to find a way back home.*

ACKNOWLEDGEMENT

Thanks to Genevieve Fisher, without whom there would be no motivation.
Thanks also to BookLeaf Publishing, who threw me a very nice-looking ad.

Miss Communication

You were astonished from the beginning at what
I could create.
I remember it as though I'd been there – the
rickety wooden house I described,
The artefacts my hero sifted through to try to
solve a mystery –
The sea-breeze howling through the broken
windows,
The uncut tufty grass waving idly outside the
drab brown walls.
Neither of us really walked there, and I never
finished the story.
Is that why you retain no patience for me now?
When I began to write poetry, I wrote with
structure.
I wrote with meter and rhyme and hoped for the
Beautiful –
That I would meet her –
And now, tired, forlorn, and lost, I fall out of the
structure.
Alliteration and assonance splinter and fester in
my words –
If I'm going to say anything at all, I want to say
it prettily –

And through my desire to impress you still
further
I think I lost the ability to share my untrod
places with you at all.
The darkest day has come upon us, now.
The claws of evil reach for us somehow,
And suddenly it matters if the unlocked door has
swung.
Because I could not share with you the tales,
My skill at weaving truth together fails.
I know you want to listen, but I cannot speak
your tongue.

Fourteen

She knew very little but said far too much.
The simplest emotions were hot to the touch.
The water was cooler, the sky just seemed bluer
—

As wrong as she was, I cannot quite rue her.

Kroger Birds

Under a violent violet sky
Next to the freeway, where cars hurtle by
Next to the store 'round about which they fly,
The Kroger Birds are home.
They're grackles and pigeons, they're gray and
coal-black,
They fly far away but they make their way back,
For despite the strange choice of a Kroger, the
fact
Is this place is their roost.
And when they convene, as they do, they, as one
–
In convection-like patterns that tend toward the
sun –
They fly and they flock and, as if just for fun,
They loop around the place.
We're like the Kroger birds – though it seems
strange,
We live in this city that's not in our range,
And flock all together – downtown breathes us
in
Then exhales us out in a group.
I won't deny there's more peace to be had
Where life moves so slow folk forget to be sad –
But being a Kroger bird isn't so bad
So long as I've got you.

Fifteen

I placed my hand on one side of the glass
And he rose to meet it, just after class.
My teeth hurt, my heart hurt – I finally knew
That I was mistaken. I tried to stay true.

Sixteen

Rolling dice and closing eyes, summers hot and
long –
Wisdom dearly gained by watching other folks
do wrong.
Great surprises, strange mirages, stories merged
to one –
Letters written to a child who had not yet come.

Stack the Dishes

My father is a rather quiet man.
His voice gets louder, though, whenever he
sings.
Favoring my mother though I am,
I have his eyes. They're deep and dark and
warm.

The kitchen in my father's mother's house
Is colored brown on walls and floor and stuffed
With spices, glasses, plates, and nice decor -
The knick-knacks of two lives, and both
well-lived.

The dual sink is on the southern wall.
Rosemary grows in cups atop the sill.
The towels are quite thin and palest white.
A little window brings into the light

Little plates on top of little plates -
Big bowls all together in a stack -
Little bowls beside them, back to back -
Silverware haphazardly beneath.

Of course the dishes cannot stack themselves.
I wondered how they'd come to be that way.

It took a couple months, but one fine day
When we had gone for dinner, I saw Dad

Calmly placing bowls on top of bowls
And scraping scraps into the bin below.
He cleaned his mother's kitchen all unasked.
My father's love was quiet, but it shone.

I was at my mother's mother's house.
Dinner was delectable - and then,
I went to put my dishes in the sink,
And saw a stack of other plates. Before

I knew what I was doing, back to back
Were little plates upon the little plates
And little bowls upon the little bowls
And silverware haphazardly beneath.

Seventeen

Have you ever felt a strange glass wall
Between yourself and others that they do not see
at all?
I saw but did not want to see. I could not yet
receive,
So though I begged for it from God, I did not
fully, yet, perceive.

Slough

Did anybody other than me graduate in Yoda
socks?
(I think that's delightful, like an ornate wall of
golden clocks).
Behind me lies a mountain view,
Before me lies a sunlit slough,
And honestly? It's hard to think, and harder to
believe.

The mountain view is clouded – storms are
forming right below my feet.
Memorials and markers tell of ancient soldiers'
sad defeat.
The trails are rough and ill-maintained,
The planks below my feet are stained,
And I was happy when at length the time had
come to leave.

The slough before me? Sure, it's wet, and I will
need some better shoes –
But with the help of those around me, I know
well I cannot lose.
The water in the slough glows gold.
The songs I'm singing won't get old.

They'll be rebaptized through the threads of
stories that we weave.

Eighteen

Harsh sounds, harsh lights, harsh times -
Lonely in good company -
I'd resolved to solve
Problems that were not my own -
Before I'd even made a move, the
Opportunity was lost.

Renew

"The creek's been dry for years," that's what you
said,
But down at the forbidden riverbed
We splashed and laughed and stumbled over
stones
While thunder hummed in distant, rumbling
tones.

You'd never looked so lovely. Dressed in green,
You seemed more tall than you had ever been.
Though nonetheless unsteady (as we knew),
You seemed to say, "I'm glad I'm here with
you."

We sat beneath the bridge and traipsed
downstream,
And largely moved in silence, like a team
That having played a game as one for years
Can move without excessive words or tears.

"My mind is darkening," that's what you said.
The flowing creek cures half of all my dread.

Nineteen

Gambling's illegal where I'm from,
But sir, I thought I'd place a bet on you.
I'm waiting over time to see it through -
This kind of long investment needs more time.

Chiaroscuro

Alliance is all he'd ever known –
That, and siphoning.
It began at the beginning, when first he had an
inkling
That he might be fit for more than darkness.
He allied himself with the burning, for he had
not the learning
To guess that the light might love him.
Misshapen and melted now,
Still aflame,
He squints at the searing sunlight
When it smiles at him.
The darkness siphons –
The flame steals –
Can light become his friend
And simply give?

Twenty

October is the cruelest month indeed.
It's strange - the eighth-turned-tenth time tends
to feed
Anxiety and things that, otherwise,
Don't generally bother with their lies.
I blame the egoistic man of old,
Who placed his name in time, and, gilt with
gold,
Created war and empire from a fall.
Oh, Julius, I blame you for it all.

Which of Us Had It Worse?

First, sister, take these stones I've carried all
these years
And weigh them in your palms. Then think of
hopes and dreams and fears
And then you may go on explaining how you are
alone.
(Sister, you and I share pasts – and grief and
blood and bone.)
Hand me, now, your heavy stones (you have
them, just as I,)
And I will lift and test their weight, and they
may make me cry,
And that's all right. I won't complain. You never
really have.
I hope you'll see we're both still here, and then
you'll start to laugh.

Twenty-One

A year before, I spied the darkest clouds
On the sky's horizon, thick, in crowds.
When I was twenty-one, I lost the trust
That you would stay the course, do what you
must.
The chair I have still testifies to you,
That though life wears its strangest face, you're
true -
But now between the hope and dread I wait,
And pray that I will not succumb to fate.

The Place That Is Not

Asaidia, I did not summon you,
Nor did I call you,
Nor did I craft you.
I was born with you engraved upon my heart.

The expansive golden fields over which the
battles flowed
'Tween nations always wrestling, reaping
whirlwinds that they sowed -
Noble northern Lassau, of the mountains high
and steep, and
Kolka of the forests and the rivers wide and
deep:
Taria dwelt in-between - the dancing diplomat,
Who had to keep both sides appeased or face
their end. Though that
Implies alliances that cannot cease to shift and
change,
She was ruled by noble houses - people good
and strange.

Mirambica was to the south, a land of plains and
tribes -
Famous for the fruits they grew and peerless
songs - and gibes,

While Essia was desert, mostly, and the westen
coast.
Her turbaned traders' mysteries were their
primary boast.
These lands, so proud and beautiful, are all
Asaidian.
If I'm lucky, I'll come back, and tell their tales
again.

Twenty-Two

My brothers sang at midnight, voices low.
The darkest day held off. but time would show
Lighthouses blazing forth are dark inside.
I'll realize, sometime soon, that I can't hide.

The Prefix An

"Doesn't that seem strange, that they're only
found here?"
-guarded against this text, you will not read it,
for
You will not admit
-antithoughts
-antithetical things to your system.
Antediluvian nonsense isn't on your menu.
Is it wrong that it's on mine?

Finite Resignation

I can't keep my hands out of my hair when it's
clean,
Which means it doesn't stay clean very long.
My socks are wet. Again.
(Trepomai.)

I pack extras. I'm resigned to the fact – if I go
out in the rain, my socks get wet.
Am I compensating for my flaws, or inviting
them?
(Trepomai).

No matter how I try to keep to higher ground,
puddles find my feet.
No matter what I do to keep myself warm, the
wind intrudes, and I quake.
It's hard to tread good paths when every path is
semi-corrupted – a semi-conductor of darkness –
a semi-clouded sky at best.
(Trepomai).

I tried to turn to a drier route.
I turned around again.
I turned a third time and was back where I'd
begun.

Hermits and ascetics don't walk in the rain, they
sit in it.
They remain stationary, and in so doing, avoid
puddles.

I ask: Is there any way to keep my socks dry (is
there any way to keep from falling again)?
He replies: Honey, there are only two ways. You
either stop going out, or you get better shoes.